PRICE: $19.95 (6989/04   )

THE LANDING

The Landing

Mark Sinnett

HARBINGER POETRY SERIES
an imprint of
CARLETON UNIVERSITY PRESS

© Mark Sinnett and
Carleton University Press Inc. 1997

Printed and bound in Canada

Canadian Cataloguing in Publication Data

Sinnett, Mark, 1963-
    The landing

(Harbinger poetry series ; 4)
ISBN 0-88629-324-3

    I. Title. II. Series.

PS8587.I563L35 1997   C811'.54   C97-900474-8
PR9199.3.S5358L35 1997

Cover design: Barbara Cumming, Carleton University Press

Front cover art, "Staircase," mixed media, Lori Richards, 1997. Courtesy Alison Holt and Innes Van Nostrand.

Carleton University Press gratefully acknowledges the support extended to its publishing program by the Canada Council and the financial assistance of the Ontario Arts Council. The Press would also like to thank the Department of Canadian Heritage, Government of Ontario through the Ministry of Culture, Tourism and Recreation, for their assistance.

Harbinger Poetry Series, Number 4

This book is for Jane

ACKNOWLEDGEMENTS

It's been a while, but I would like to thank the old *F* and *Grind* gang for their influence and generosity. That means Sue-Ellen Gerritsen, Andy Griffin, Deirdre Hanna, François Lachance, Caroline Newton and Chris Wooding. I also owe much gratitude to Victor Coleman, who pointed out the fork in the road.

Thanks as well to Mary Cameron and Kent Nussey, who read parts of the manuscript. And especially to Steve "The Hitman" Heighton. He was good enough to scrutinize the whole thing, and his suggestions make this a better book. Chris Levenson, my editor, was unfailingly generous with his time and talent. Thanks to Christine LeBlanc at C.U. Press, and to Lori Richards for providing the glorious artwork.

Jane Lafarga makes all the difference, and she deserves her own paragraph.

I wish also to acknowledge the support of the Canada Council. Earlier versions of some of these poems appeared in *The Antigonish Review, Carousel, The Last Word* (Insomniac Press, 1995), *The Literary Review of Canada, The Nashwaak Review, Quarry,* and *Vintage 94* (Quarry Press, 1995). Cheers to all the editors.

CONTENTS

WOOL SWEATERS

map 2
wool sweater 4
breakwater 5
before what we did 6
late riser 7
over time, over space 10
time delay 11
what to think I don't know 13
two reasons you will hate me 14
espresso 15
mother and daughter 17
plums 19

CITIES

soaps 22
digging graves 23
no strings 24
the neighbours 25
condensations 27
olives at John's 28
hawk 29
the wading pool 30
on the bike 31
brain surgery 33

POLAROIDS

home court advantage 36
the more distant limbs 38
pictures in what the river left 40

checking up on Gould   41
the new forest   43
brain   45
east   46

LANDSCAPES

a new record   48
gold rush   49
with open mind   50
a new plot   51
tracking in mud   53
prison break   56
doubting Thomas   57
we rattle north   58

WOOL SWEATERS

MAP

    Already the second day,
                       and yet now I know
only that the smaller road
flails away from the highway
                    like ribbon —

a way north built without compass
laid down before the geography of stars,
when language was only a chaos
                    of sound.

Somewhere along the edge of that stretch
they will find you.

I have sent out the scouts,
those sniffers of violet, soap, and mood,
told them to deduce your path,
                        sloping back I suspect
to water.

                More likely
they will discover you
through my remains, the scent I left
at the top of your arm,

or the slight breath
you took from our heat,
                      and keep still
at the bottom of your lungs,
a weight you cannot shed
                    without running.

I have equipped these searchers
with the strong lights of miners
and told them to search
all night, to follow the eyes
at the road's spine.

Go north, I said,
                to deep water
for it is in those places
she goes to dance.

WOOL SWEATER

I don't know what it is.

The way you pull it over
your head maybe, your body
so lean in its stretching. Or
the two rows of bone there
that frame my gasps like a grammar,
describe better than I
the way I stutter down stairs.

Even the way bright wool
is pulled to transparency
over your cheekbones; the world
become all angles & dark
for you, askew and Caligari.

All these drive me mad.

So wrapped though, you are blind
to me (and where I stand for this
movie), miss altogether how
I point at you from a room's
shadowed edge, say:

> 'There, maybe her throat
> then was a symbol,' or
> 'There — see the slim vase
> she has made of her arms?'

how, conspiring,
I nudge the space around me.

BREAKWATER

You, the American
girl with feet

which ran over the rocks
like water, never quite

so fast that we could
say you were falling,

but always on the edge
of something unpractised —

a look over your shoulder
a hand to your face

the way your breasts went
briefly with your sweater

and then fell away, static
electricity burning in you

and your hair, as you
changed clothes in that

high room under the low roof
then asked me to stay;

made like nothing else
ever happened in this city —

let me stand there amazed
listening to the chatter

in the telephone wires
as they slapped against the window.

BEFORE WHAT WE DID

we fell back together
against rocks, you
flattening like a sheet

able to take to
almost any bed, it
seemed like something

out of myth, your legs
this sudden buffer
against granite, your

hands white, and bent
like gulls — arched
for flight, fingers

that pointed home.

LATE RISER

You wait up so late
for the bread to rise, needing
more time than you thought
because the house — though it is summer —
is also brick and much cooler
than any oven our neighbours
imagine we live in.

You change from radio station
to TV channel, your energies
now flagging.

*

The loaf, two dozen buns
are in another room, like the English
downs under the green tea towels
your mother gave us. Though
now they have started —
in the time it has taken me
to write this — to rise above
the red rim of the bowl,
the steel lip of the tray
you folded that one lump
over, seems like hours ago.

*

Soon, you say to me,
Soon ...

before I give up on you,
count the stairs under
my breath as I climb.

*

You will wait for that bread,
I know, whether it is ready
in an hour, hard and hollow
to your knock

or whether it takes you on
past the last show, the end
of Tuesday's late movie.

You will wait,
even though I might finish
every book in the house
waiting for you ...

*

And when you do come up to me,
in the end, swinging your arms
in the room's air
with a rough semaphore
that says you want me
to be proud of you,
pushing around the smells
of yeast, of baking, stirring them
about you until they are over me
like a blanket

I am awake enough only
to cover you, to see that
flour has somehow found the back
of your neck, is a fog in the fine
hair at the top of your spine

*

and I lie there in the gusts
of memory brought on by your scent —
those of the oven door closing
the library's opening

before I loose myself
from your body, untie
the knots we made

and turn instead to the bright,
bitter marmalades I grew up with;
the soft, warm butter.

OVER TIME, OVER SPACE

Something in my mind, the way
(you smile)
the match flickers as I
light the flames, breathe smoke

swim in deep torrents
(of you, your hair)
and am burned away
by Greyhounds.

It isn't just
(memory)
but a primitive instant, charcoal
etchings of what we are.

I draw ash from
(that fire)
recreate old moments
from time before the mountains

ranged between us
(still, strong)
and then I see you
through these mirrors

of far-eastern cities
(that stem from the fiery
brook) and the towers of old
Montreal.

TIME DELAY

Every day it is harder to
not make this thing we have
more permanent,

your dismay become so
evident in the fetid clumping
of our bedsheets, your brown

arms knotted angrily,
and even your toes curled
as if to make a fist

keeping me away. Now
only weather systems
bring any humidity

to our lives, a heat. *We need ...
oh, I don't know*, you say,
knowing full well. *We*

are missing something.
What you mean is I am
supposed to have asked

for your hand by now,
found my courage.
Even this edging past

euphemisms (this *thing*
we have, for example)
is enough, though,

to start some mental
centrifuge, spin out
the idea of children

who resemble one
or the other of us.
Already I hear them

in the street. And
it frightens me, how
fast they run away

with any inclination
I have to write more
poetry, mean something.

WHAT TO THINK I DON'T KNOW

It was you, the sight of you,
                    like birds,
caught so fleeting in this
peripheral net — a flash of wing,
sweat of net handlers,
a flat rain in our face.

I sat way down
past the maypole, you wouldn't
have seen me, that riot
of colours twisted
against blue sky,
braided soon
              like hair,
obscuring everything ...

I watched from beneath the pool
as if you were flight and I
some sunken swimmer

Held you in my hands
                  — in my mind —
wiped the road from your arms
your hips; changed the light
on your bike
and watched you go.

TWO REASONS YOU WILL HATE ME

I

You will hate me
because we had friends
over without discussing it
first

and because I have frozen
the soft raspberries you wanted
to give them after dinner
                            even though they leered at you
over coffee, their subtly angled
teaspoons making them look
like drunken dentists, men who have
mistaken your leg for a molar,
your chair for a brace.

II

You will hate me
because I have told them all
what you can do to chocolate
with your tongue,

                    how you have
made a complete chess set
from the white Swiss and darker Belgian
chocolates you were given
at the reception.

If it is any consolation
(and I know it will be)
they were particularly impressed
by the sixteen pawns
you whipped off in a weekend.

ESPRESSO

I camp out in this sad-sack café,
its low paisley sofa, blue box of news.

I've done it for days. To watch you
carry slick Caesar salads, bloody
celeried Caesars to that window table
slop Creemore creamy over the bar
your blue pinafore sailing out behind
thin pale legs, frail sandals
they don't make any more.

Then Hereyouarehereyouarehereyouare
weeding the bulletin board, tending
that origami garden beside me.
You pull a rainbow of push pins
drop them tinkling into chipped glass
sugar-packet bowl, make the cork slate
between us clean, as it were.
Then replace in tile pattern:

announcements for dance recitals, readings
yoga classes, a call for subjects
at a campus sleep lab. The wall
become Kandinsky and then some.
And there you go.

I distract myself with the horrid
still lifes, weepy watercolours
I reviewed for our weekly and hated.
Wonder if the artist sits here
day in day out, watches us watching
his work (that old game). As if.

By day five I am extrapolating
from your tired greying smile
furred turtleneck. I see the rumpled
orange shag of your room, a rust-stained
triangle of floorbound futon where

limp sheets have pulled away.
Columns of butt ash on the counter
toast crumbs burnt and brushed
onto the windowsill. Aloe plant
scarred with fingernail crescents.
A procession of lint-bellied men
hoarding still-sticky-with-you fingers.

This is how I remain faithful.
I stay away long enough.

MOTHER AND DAUGHTER

So many times
I have ascribed emotions to you
for the sake of image, language,

or even just the odd phrase, anything
to get my name in the papers.

I have told them that
you ran away with my daughter
when you only took her to the fair,

taught her how to take photographs
by starlight —

the ferris wheel and water slides,
now these arcing skids of colour
on paper that has learned some way
to collect them ...

*

In fact you almost drowned
in her odd sorrows,
and would as soon tumble after her
                                  like weed,
trail wide grass cuts through
those bright fields she loved,
those of mustard
                and wheat,

and then fall, clumsy and damp
against the sharpness of tree bark,
your legs bared to the winds
all around you,
                admiring your handiwork

as you would wait here with me
and that picture you took

of our daughter.

PLUMS

There is, I think, fruit
on the countertop
and (though it is dark)

it is most likely a bowl
                        — round
and full of plums.

I imagine they must be over-
ripe by now (you see I remember
how long ago you bought them)

but from here they look (still)
for all the world like
tiny perfect muscles — cut away
from the body and pumped up
full of blood.

Someone else has been here
too, because there are others —
peeled already and apart,
with flesh the colours of a bruise

flesh that has collapsed
under its own weight and will
slide over the tongue
                        like an egg.

If I'm right it was you
who moved down here
                        through night
thick as treacle, came here
ahead of me

then sucked the stones free, your cheeks
drawn in like small caves
washed smooth and white by the sea.

And those are your eyes now
on the other side of the table
								laughing at me,
creased up by the small steps I take
towards you, the way I stumble
over my words.

CITIES

SOAPS

Jane is amazed. *I'm always amazed,*
she says, *how people come home
on the soap operas. They throw off
coats, grab at an apple, the mail, anything
to chew on heading for the bathroom
or to change.*

(I nod, wait.) *And then they close
the door behind them,* she says.
*No one in the real world does that,
right? I mean, who's going to see them?
Don't they realize this gives the burglar
time to escape, the sick gloved murderer*

a chance to plant poisons?
(Doesn't she know this is a lot
of rhetorical questions to use up
at once?) *It isn't human to do that.
It jars,* she tells me, *I'm knocked out
of the world when it's written that way.*

I tell Jane she's right, it's a failing,
but not to get excited. *Leave it alone,
this is "Melrose Place" and it happens
all the time.* She snorts at me;
when the commercials come she heads
to the bathroom (the door left wide)

and I hear everything she does, even
over Amanda's screaming for Billy
to get the hell out, throwing something
— I don't know what — at him,
its slow arc defying the laws of physics.

DIGGING GRAVES

Your brother is over, a new girlfriend
with him. They don't act
the way we do together.

It is affection that
defines them,
not the affectations we have
gathered around us like antiques.
Tonight I slip outside rather than
eat dinner with the three of you.

Hard stuff to digest — the notion
rot has set in with its heady stink
and sensation of alcohol, rough mead
we've made by pulling apart.
A new destructive chemistry.

We watch televisions in different
rooms, or else from the upstairs windows
see other people we might have
got along with.

I move under the one plum tree
spared by blight arrived to build
in our garden. I scratch desperate,
animal, at the ground. For what,
though? Memento, bus fare?

My whole body is involved, seizes
at an activity which slows down
the mind, this beginning of a tunnel
take me I hope the hell out of here
and probably right behind me
you too.

NO STRINGS

In the morning, you
in the shower, and the needle
still ticking in a new groove

worn on the inner edge
of the record you said you loved

and yet couldn't name a song from,
the first of many lies ...

I find one earring
caught in the bed spread,

spinning free as I swing
for the ground. A tiny metal kite
in a green flannel sky.

THE NEIGHBOURS

They have taken their lawn
away, which is an awkward way
of saying it is gone, that

they have rolled out concrete
instead, a thick white pastry
under which myriad roots

must (this was done last year)
have learnt to fight that urge
requiring them to move

towards light — the wild tropism
I learnt about in England.
One of many urges I thought

I shared with the slim
greenery we slapped between glass
slides, then magnified many

hundred times (I saw chaos
backlit there, its intricate moving
surface). I wouldn't want to examine

too closely, either, the way
I watched their daughter walk
over that white acreage (she was

young, she could have been
from the university, my age
would frighten her. And her

parents). Or speculate on why
I looked at — hell, ogled —
her feet, made my mind do

extraordinary tasks
separating her shoes
from the shadows they touched

with every light step, beyond
saying I hoped she might sink
a little into the walkway,

be preserved there for me
— which is undoubtedly why
they poured this hard field

while she was at school, out
— they thought — of harm's way.
And why they smile at me now

even though the way she walks
is so plain to see. There are,
and they believe this, no traps

for her to fall into. Their world
is rock solid like this, without
the yellowed and patchwork lawn,

its many uncharted footfalls.

CONDENSATIONS

Have you ever looked back at us
through the plastic windows we blow on
to the frames in winter,
gluing them down so tight?

It's possible you would
see the two of us,
moving from room to room
like gunslingers, provoking
different landscapes of mist
over each clearing sheet

the collapse of mountains
without cliff, the movement
of rivers to estuary
                    and then salt
... sometimes the shapes
of entire continents

and what must be oceans,
with all the depth of our flurried garden
(though their shape is less
familiar to us than these lands
we have created from need).

There is also this pattern of fence,
drawn over the snow like a comb
or the lines on a map —
latitudes I have given myself
to keep going, a way of keeping track
of the noise. And the shapes
I keep mistaking for you,
beneath the heavy trees.

OLIVES AT JOHN'S

On Sunday at John's Deli, and
lost for anything else,
I talked of olives

bored you with detail,
and so disguised my lack
of ideas. I moved on to

the acidity of soil, and
(by angling my arms) drew out
the treacherous dry slopes

those trees grow on. All this
while cradling the fruit
as if precious to me,

new teeth for a perfect jaw.
As you stood there too,
telling me of a new book

its second printing, and all
the dirt needed to make it
bloom. Your wool hat was wet

under the lights. Outside
the store, snow climbed higher
than brickwork the windows

sat on; deep tracks we made
getting here were full or else
faded into background.

HAWK

My coffee's gone grey, the biscuits
hard. I'm in a mood — pale, milky,
staring at lines for Christmas tax
refunds, Sally Anners, headbangers
and country singers. Haggards
siring Vedders. Some gawkers stop,
then figure it out and dart.

Last night it was beasts, elephants
stomping among smooth-skinned
trees, arms nearly, a dreamgrove
must be out of Jung seeing how
Jane saw them too, accepted
they might be.

Maybe the high was due
to gifts exchanged, new friends
come good. The phone talk of warmth
giving us the shivers (you
give me Chivas). And music
wringing the same delusions out
of us all. Waits. That man
is a drug in us sometimes.

They could use some in that
line. Drag out speakers, Man.
Music's too loud in here anyway,
coffee's none too hot either
and I feel the spirit move me
to it, the vision I condescend to
experiment with, their lives
skeins anyway, balls fat cats
play with.

I watch my bike out there
like a hawk too, its shiny metal
like wrapping paper, like
a hooker's dress, young girl.

THE WADING POOL

The wading pool, its skin-thick water set
deep into concrete basin, going green
with algae, brings me here. To a park cut
out of old cemetery, graves now swung
or swum over oblivious. I kick
at the ground, though, dislodge from clay thin-boned
shin, a doctor's back tooth, and keep an eye
on the lifeguard who thinks writing a trick,
these words a twisted rope just now wound
to lure her away. In the shade I try
to arrange my body to reflect hers,
its look as unconscious of form as those
children she protects, the splashing monsters
her moves grow from: the jutted hip, few clothes.

ON THE BIKE

Six swimmers slick, near gelatinous
from the water. Two are entangled
in lengths of weed, growths
tumorous on them — burned pearls
much darker than water, even deep
water. *Like rope* the taller says, looping
great strands about her. A green
moving curtain of water. Gift wrap.

Second time around (I lap the city)
they are dressed, engaged in series
of Tai Chi movements — auras full
of phosphorous, distant blinking
stars. The lake is background here,
just an illustration of effects
not fully grasped. Pictures like these
adorn tabloids — none of them, though,
so untouched by airbrush.

I have friends who want to move out
this way. I tell them be careful,
admit that I am grateful for any speed
I derive from hills beforehand,
and save energy for this slip
down into floodplain.

The smell from the water plant
is bad sometimes, casts acrid nets
over brick row houses Jane wants one of,
An end one, she says. Their worthless
view of the islands. It is a smell
I thought we had left behind,
our technologies overcoming it.

You had better warn them, she says
*not to swim in the water. Or else
to carry knives like those divers
strap to the inside of a calf.*

*Have them practice rituals at lakeside,
their feet draped awkwardly over
ruby-veined rocks like handcloths.
Tell them it is important. Tell them
they are our friends.*

BRAIN SURGERY

On the TV I have just watched surgery
where the skull is hacked apart
by bright chisel and the smash
of sterile hammer.

Bone chips spun towards the camera
like sleet, or arrow heads
in miniature, rough white needles
they would surely need
                      for the reassembly.

Through it all
            a woman slept, her face
peeled over high cheekbones, but *downwards*,
towards her mouth, resting
in the surgeon's hands, two holes
where the eyes should be,
one more — and bigger — for the nose.

There seems no way for any body to recover
from such indignity, for the face to
fit the skull again, to get over
the bone's exposure to the elements,
for a mouth to figure out smiling.

*

When it was done, I drank
the last of the beers we had bought
for the weekend, stared into the sun
until I was sure they would never do this
to me, and then sat there — numb,
waiting for the anaesthetic to wear off.

POLAROIDS

HOME COURT ADVANTAGE

As kids it felt we were always rooting
among the skeletal bottom limbs
of fir trees huddled thick around
that court, shoving aside branches
with wrecked wooden racquets (we had
no use yet for graphite) in a search
for balls lost in long third sets
— fatigue upon us like a storm,
making us clumsy. Surrounding fences
were worn thin, gone in spots,
and some of the hardest-hit balls
punched right through. They changed
shape — were American footballs
and then resembled hourglass.

Nowadays, a computer can do this,
slow it all down and prove it —
the break-down of a man's fitness,
the physical properties of rubber
and lemon-felt when softened in heat —
show in grim detail whatever's
too quick for the eye. Render it all
in 3-D. Even the long skids
provoked by well-hit backhands, low
rushing clouds of red-tinged dust,
are made visible, lively, on the screen.

You forget sometimes, I forget,
even England has a climate capable
of doing this to a man / woman /
boy/girl: wilting them, bringing them
to their knees. The groundskeeper there
used heavy sprays to settle the clay down
and reveal gentle slopes on-court.
He was the source of infinitely small
river systems, and he thought himself God.

Strange, though, that the importance of this
memory — a school tennis court grown
unruly, overgrown with fir trees
that shook brittle limbs at us
like the barbed stingers of wasps —
cannot be named beyond this
wordy show of its prominence, the way
it is woven, a repetitive dark pattern,
into all these mental nets.

THE MORE DISTANT LIMBS

In England then deeper, to Oxford,
where the botanical gardens fan
between thin brown ribbons, tributaries
poured from the River Thames: Isis,
Cherwell, and one other (I think),
one I won't remember again.

The muddy weed-full waters swing lazily
around stained boat houses; support
legion wooden punts drifting punters
like me. They make magnetic patterns
of the leaves — slim pale lemons, figshapes
let fall by willow trees leaning over
their banks. Offer burials off land
to the odd cricket ball lofted for six
over the walkway, motley anglers.

Everything looks to come full circle
at the rural edge of a city
I happened to grow up in.

Most vivid now is the wild humidity
in those greenhouses (over there
we say it is 'close,' the weather
where water is hung out to dry
in the air) and tiny dimpled oranges
set forever against the more distant
limbs of rubber plants. I see them
still in my sleep.

I wanted to steal that fruit and spirit
away to the Isis' sharp-sloped banks,
peel the electric skin and discard it
like a snake's jacket in the long dark
curve of water. To consume the flesh
recklessly.

But now, when I think so criminally,
the river is dyed, rendered brilliant
but bitter within its muscle. Sharp rings
roll out from the incident like radar
(such sweet nostalgia!) and wash eventually
to Canadian shores — rare amber tides
I will write about for years.

PICTURES IN WHAT THE RIVER LEFT

As in a dream

    where the air is full
    of the tiniest fish imaginable
    all come ashore to feed

    and everyone covers their mouth,
    tries desperately not to
    breathe them in

this new route to the roof
is a dark one, one of coal
now, rather than wood

as if evolution has all of a sudden
been reduced to this

one last transformation
at speed.

CHECKING UP ON GOULD

His thin thin hands.

I had seen them before, but
not so still, or long enough
to really appreciate them, to
study all the joints. Find,
in other words, a dozen new reasons
for the ways they moved.

I can only imagine
the machine they must have
wheeled in to the room
for that last shot of his hands' bones:
the lengthy x-ray that showed knuckles
dancing like puppets in front of
grey walls — disjointed, a touch mad.

The room mapped out:

The Steinway   the x-ray machine
    the french sliding doors

        & out
      to a patio
     he often walked
    ... in soft shoes

those early footfalls
like a series of plums
dropped into sand.

It seems too technical, in the end,
so cold a machine in a room
so warm, wallpaper like the skin
from peaches, a fur peeled slow
& arranged into subtle pattern.
To say, when the camera has hummed
down into silence, 'Now play
something, something dramatic.'

Perhaps instead they had him go right
into the hospital, directed him
from behind stiff leaden curtains.
Or else these are not his hands at all,
and those fingers that scuttle about
in that celluloid wash like crabs
are those of a stand-in.

Maybe a woman did this,
or else just someone
the director found by chance, a man
drumming his fingers on a windowsill,
watching the clock and waiting
for a word — any word — from doctors
who have learnt some way to lean
against the air, to stand completely still
in their long ivory jackets.

THE NEW FOREST

For Hope

I

Her infant back is bent
as if by a blacksmith's tools

hammer   anvil   fire

steel so suddenly chilled
it scales in the cooling
tank like fish, assumes

the arcs of rupture,
of earthquake.

There is no settling for this
position,
        a sense grows in us

that even metal was never meant
to assume this form.

II

And the logging of bones
by grey machine

                (quiet photographs
that show her skeleton
            soft
as the stems of plants,
              but blown out of line
by some busted gene, her spine
curled like a hair on the negative
                  and thick
between her ribs)

disturbs me, becomes in the doctor's mouth
just a mess of new words
      dark maps
of a city without commerce, roads
full of blood, and beyond
understanding.

III

But the day this cast is cut away,
         thrown out,
and the saw has stopped, is stilled
behind those curtains
that swing around her
      like storms,
desolate with the sounds of metal
runners and plastic sheet,

the rain will find new ways
over her body,
     drain over muscles
as if over stones
in the bed of a new river,

burnish her skin,
      and then fall away
with the plaster,

     carry the white dust
between far northern hills

       and leave it there.

BRAIN

And in this bit of my head, as I get it,
a micro-volt illuminates space,
telegraphs across something gelatinous,
grey, triggers the desire I have
to recall, to write this.

But it's more: a foggy-day world of frontier towns
dense with disciplined gunmen
blasting each other discriminately.

Take that. And that. I marshall
these unseen elements with a weakening grip.
*Lame duck, lion's cage, give it up,
skinny boy.* They feed me this stuff.

In school we cut through a pig's head
with hacksaw, elbow grease. Dandruff of bone.
Rolled its blueish lobes, snipped-away eyes, in our hands,
Billy Corgan saying *Can you read my palm now,
sucker?*
      I have that smell in me still:
brain remembering a lesser
dimmer brain,
and gloating.

EAST

I am sure I remember you
writing of blossoms
              — something about plums
in a garden. Perhaps you were teaching
nearby, although this map
              is unclear;
rain has turned all the streets into lines
drawn as if by an errant plough
                that lurches
over a dark, rocky field.

There was an explosion too, I think,
and if I went for your books now
I would soon find the piece,
            the page still folded over,
hiding the first line.

It was a short scene, little more
than a spasm of memory,
            yours
              and now mine,
sharply focused but
with no sound.

It made me feel as if
we could only talk to each other
              through very old films.

LANDSCAPES

A NEW RECORD

On the weekend, away
from the Smashing
Pumpkins record
you just bought — and wouldn't leave
alone in the city —
we split wood for hours; sweat
ran over the axe handle
to frozen ground.

We were at your cottage
sorting out fire
wood from the rotting pine
stumps that hide soft honey-
combs at their centres.

Those are no good for the house,
there is no heat in them,
they are just dry
geometries crumbling
to dandruff snow in the wake
of arcing blade —

like ideas not worth saving
for poetry, follies that strain
to outdo oceans, devolve
into new shapes more worthy
of our attention, to ruins.

GOLD RUSH

You died,

and in sorting things we found maps
in lace-lined drawers beside your bed.
They were stained with tea or else,
we decided, were old as the hills.

Somewhat more remote
was the possibility you baked
the paper to this brittle state,
and honest to that notion

we inspected cookie trays
like Columbo (a quick search
we emerged from moody).
The path shown was known to us;

it ran around back of barns
that as kids we hid in,
learning to make rhymes.
And it led — past thick stream, over-

hanging willow — to graves
beyond the churchyard's wall,
three mounds little more
risen than camber, and too short,

we thought, for other than dogs.
We came to dig, though, and did —
past dark, the stone wall swung
around us like cloak, air

become by night wet, heavier
than the bones we threw white
into the sky, and which — in so arcing —
were animate and a treasure to us.

WITH OPEN MIND

There are no fish here
though elsewhere they swim
in huge numbers

and push the water
(through their collective movement)
to a pool some place else, some-
where beyond words and the trees
we sit around all day drinking.

In the end it all tails off

                            — our thin line
of stories and the water that made it
here okay, if a little muddied —

into shadow and a damp pasture
full of footprints. Our clothes
are thrown about here too
— though everyone closes their eyes
and doesn't notice how

they collect wetness from beneath
themselves, long like lapping tongues.

A NEW PLOT

I forget, fired up this way
as if by slingshot on the weekends
(unwitting car in a train

full of bright metal that speeds
at mental rates north
toward cottage or else estate, some

decrepit run-down hunting camp),
that more die here
than too-slow deer, red

squirrels, the jellied pike
gill-ripped on rocks spreading
like a pale pink linen

around Head Lake. And that
in the cemetery we planned
to explore — there was talk of tracing

paper and stone rubbings,
though what would we have done with them? —
a new plot has appeared

quilted with marigold, clumps of
delphinium which rise from the bedding
plants like ragged plumes of a heartbeat,

the colour of old veins.
(Predictably, we imagined the grave
a child's, not someone more aged,

rheumatic, more
willing to go.) The living
around here must make

efforts to bury those who die
mid-week, I think, when
they have the place to themselves

and it is quiet again.
But lakeside all this is gone.
New skis thump free, noisy

against the surface. There is the smell
of meat. And any mention of death
shocks me to no end.

TRACKING IN MUD

We wake up to depths of snow
like winter catalogues

scenes I never dreamed of
in England — and Wales,
where I studied
the formations of estuary

and depression
in mining towns that tumbled
down hill sides ramshackle
and blackened,

fell off the new maps
altogether.

*

I have but one memory of ice
in those countries.

It is of barrel-chested carp,
                      huge fish
deeper than the water
they tried to live in

and how they swam at odd angles
when the laketops froze,
dorsal fins rubbing
against hard sky

and how they flooded (as if for photos)
to those places
we broke open
with rocks.

Surely *then* I must have imagined
this shield I was aimed at,

seen its enormous white weight,
my own weaknesses.

*

No? In the black-windowed pubs
then, full of old beer, and a dust
you try not to breathe.

                      Where the light points out
repetitive curves of glass
that rest on the table
like a spill,

give off some reflection
of the band.

There, where I talked up a transatlantic storm.

*

No. Never.

And here, in the Kingston kitchen
before noon
          (but twelve years in)

when I look outside
beyond the yard,
to where the sky that
describes these new allotments
has never been lower
                than this
and in our laneway
the fence is reduced
to a line of points
                like seed markers

across the ground
signposts,

I still know only
            that I should sleep for a while
and try again later
from elsewhere.

PRISON BREAK

On Sunday morning we take
a bad road north to Bellrock,
soon just gravel that skids

along shallow flood, the
trees like blown glass on
the water table, as close

to the surface as grave.
There are no children here
but surprisingly gardens

where men have stretched
thin skins of lawn over
the rock, made looms

of the land, quilted patterns
you can't see in the city:
the occasional horse, white

against the erratics, random
weak sprays of trees, cows
like sculpture; and the house

we always wanted, with its blue
tin roof for us to lie on,
write poems about the city.

DOUBTING THOMAS

Will I this way become some real arsehole
given time; have I set that mute process,
that long slide, in motion, let the sized pole
be dug in deep enough soil they could test
the measure of me? Or the ground we boot
around become so mutinous it now
reaches up for me, sending skyward god-
knows-what tendrils round old rock, past thick root
to pull me under, to silence my mouth
as I push at old age? And do I prod
such friends as hang about into dank holes
where they'll sell us good whitefish, a whole mess
of wet chips, pints of dark bitter pulled cold;
badger them silly for scotch, maybe less?

WE RATTLE NORTH

We rattle north to Sydenham. Then gather
even more heat in the village, our open
windows bricked over, ablaze with it.
But we don't stop. We head further,

through steep, near-fatal switchbacks,
to Gould Lake. In the car we are
forever veering madly, leaving
our allotted lane as if to track

over unploughed earth, thick gravel
shoulder — Jane yells to *Watch the road!*
more than once. The grass in fields
beside us sways at waist level

already. This is what I am thinking
when I straighten the car out — how
tall the grass is — my eyes fixed, hands
wet on the wheel. Its leather bringing

the scent of babies' arms, reminding me
she wants to talk more about family
when we get there. The road points sharply,
is a torturous winding. For three

miles I am rally driver, dusting hedges,
painting them in clouds of grey. My father
would be proud of me. He loves this part
of the country — *It is just like Wales*

he says, and *England was never quite
this primitive.* He means well; good
intentions spin away like the water that
flies off Jane when she climbs crab-like

from the lake soon afterwards (*This was
a good idea!*) and shakes her head
like a dog. I get a smile from behind
thick red veils of towelling; moths

flail in the upset, vacuumed air as
she flops to the flat hard fringe
before forest, slick green rock.
I don't mind even your driving, if

I can do this at the end of it,
she says. I am annoyed beyond all
reason by this; can find nothing
to explain why. I am frantic

and storm back to the car, read
yellowed newspapers all day. The sun
burns my forearms through the glass
and lets mum's words grow rampant, seed-

like in my head: *That girl, she's
nearly family to me.* This is the slim
consolation I am forced to grab at,
my buoy. A dim glint beyond trees.

HARBINGER POETRY SERIES

Harbinger Poetry Series, an imprint of Carleton University Press, is dedicated to the publication of first volumes of poetry by aspiring poets. Initially, Harbinger's mandate is to publish two volumes per year, and eventually to publish no fewer than four volumes per year. As the title of the series implies, our mission is to herald poets in whom we have discovered not just the potential for good verse, but an already clear and confident voice.

Series Editor
    Christopher Levenson

Editorial Board
    Diana Brebner
    John Flood
    Holly Kritsch
    Blaine Marchand

ALSO AVAILABLE IN THIS SERIES

Holly Kritsch, *Something I'm Supposed to Remember*
"Holly Kritsch is an immediately attractive poet, gifted with the stern voice of raw confession. Telling of harrowing blasphemies against childhood, telling of violation and irrepressible love, her poetry matters."
— *George Elliott Clarke*

Ronna Bloom, *Fear of the Ride*
"Few poets write of grief and love with such a simple elegance and an impressive depth. Ronna Bloom writes clear and hard about what hurts, and gives us hope."
— *Susan Musgrave*

Anne Le Dressay, *Sleep is a Country*
"Have you heard rocks keening? Anne Le Dressay helps us recognize the sound. Austere as ancient standing stones, her poems are perfectly shaped, perfectly positioned to reflect the wordless light."
— *Mary A. Wright*